Dogs
with
Old Man
Faces

ISBN 978-0-7624-4894-4

Library of Congress Control Number: 2013939722

E-book ISBN 978-0-7624-5066-4

9   8   7   6   5   4   3   2   1
Digit on the right indicates the number of this printing

Cover and interior design by Bill Jones
Edited by Jennifer Kasius
Typography: Myriad Pro and Bernhard Bold

Running Press Book Publishers
2300 Chestnut Street
Philadelphia, PA 19103-4371

Visit us on the web!
www.runningpress.com

Dogs
with
Old Man Faces

Portraits of
Crotchety Canines

Tom Cohen

RUNNING PRESS
PHILADELPHIA · LONDON

TACO

lost an eye
in Korea.

DUSTER

enjoys a
good knish.

MR. TIGGS

ponders the
Civil War.

MUTTLEY
is worried about the future of Medicare.

LOUIE

oft quotes classic literature.

GRUNT
is not
ashamed of
his liver spots.

JACK
enjoys a
hot cup of
Sanka.

CHEKHOV

is a former

Soviet

gymnast.

ARCHIE

is almost

always

drunk.

SAUL

remembers
a better time.

CONFETTI
is too short
to reach
the canned
peaches.

FELIX

has had
some work
done.

JACQUES

is a French wine
snob.

PRINGLES

was a bodybuilder before the arthritis.

PASCAL

was the first
male professor
of Women's
Studies.

SCAMP

bears a strong
resemblance
to Grandpa
Munster.

DIXON

is a Texas
Republican.

HARLEY

is a former
Green Beret.

SPARKY

came out

before it was

fashionable.

ROLO

once

dated

Sparky.

MR. BEAN

is an old

letch.

SCOUT
plays golf
in a kilt.

EMMITT

has a gun rack
on his pickup
truck.

RUFUS

laments
his botched
facelift.

RINGO

tears up
at the
Memorial Day
parade.

BAXTER

smoked
too much pot
in the '60s.

PEPPER

has been advised
to cut down
on salt.

CUBBY

overdosed
on Rogaine.

OLLIE

is a paranoid
doomsday
prepper.

SHERMAN

goes on
senior singles
cruises.

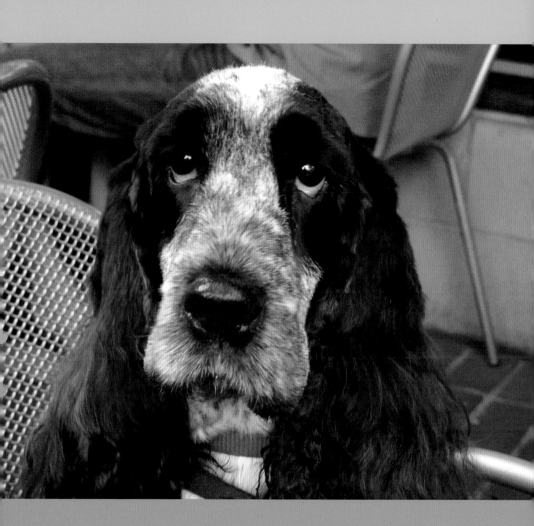

HENRY

is hostile at the chiropractor's office.

PRINCE

has that
"old person smell."

JINX

is blind

without his

bifocals.

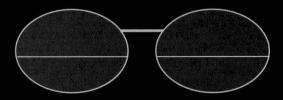

FRANK

is waiting
for the prune juice
to kick in.

TONTO
invented
the unibrow.

CHUCK

enjoys

a sponge bath

on Tuesdays.

HOMER
was once
Mao's tailor.

WHISKEY

doesn't always
drink beer,
but when he does,
he prefers
XX Dos Equis.

ROSCOE

was one of
the original
Hells Angels.

SUMO

wants those kids
off his lawn.

MARSHMALLOW

laughs at
his own
racist jokes.

GEPPETTO

is horrified
   at how much
$ things cost.

BANDIT

"medicates"
his glaucoma,
if you know
what I mean.

CHEWY

is still upset
they cancelled
Matlock.

MEATBALL

is a wrinkled
old nudist.

OTIS

has 87
godpuppies.

MAX

is pleased
with his new
dentures.

LUCKY

lost his pension
playing the slots.

Viagra
makes
SCRUFFY
very
happy.

CHOO CHOO

still rents
VHS tapes
from the library.

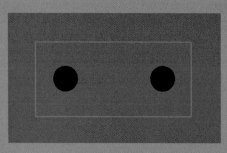

This is
COMET's
version of
assisted
living.

WIGGLES

has one
glass eye.

BARNEY

wishes
he hadn't
retired.

TANK

is a master
of Mahjong.

RASCAL

uses

Just For Men.

SPUDS

is worried
for America.

IRVING

believes in
aging
gracefully.

MUNGO

doesn't trust
anyone
under 70.

RILEY

can't wait
    for tonight's
        Early Bird Special.

BOGIE

thinks pit bulls
are ruining
the neighborhood.

ROCKY

is just a
crazy old
bastard.

GUS

got Grecian
Formula
in his eye.

just found out he's
being put in a home.

DAKOTA

still parties hard.

MONTY
represents
the 1%.

BINGO

decided
to try
collagen.

DEXTER's

back

gets hairier

with age.

BOOMER

hates his
prostate
exam.

PEDRO

likes

Old Spice

and Sinatra.

HARRY

didn't want to be in
this book but his wife
said, "Come on, Harry,
try something new
for once."

PHOTO CREDITS

Tom Cohen: Baxter, Cubby, Pepper, Ollie, Sherman, Henry, Prince, Jinx, Archie, Confetti, Pascal, Roscoe, Choo Choo, Monty, Bingo, Dexter

Dan Winters: Taco, Louie, Jack, Saul, Emmitt, Felix, Scamp, Scout, Ringo, Sumo, Marshmallow, Gepetto, Bandit, Chewy, Meatball, Otis, Lucky, Scruffy, Tank, Mungo, Riley, Bogie, Rocky, Gus, Oreo, Boomer, Pedro, Mr. Tiggs

T.J. Nuckolls, www.sxc.hu photo: Duster

Richard Dudley, www.sxc.hu photo: Muttley, Frank

Claudia Meyer, www.sxc.hu photo: Grunt

JM, www.sxc.hu photo: Chekhov

Renato Cardoso, www.sxc.hu photo: Jacques

Bob MacInnes, www.flickr.com: Pringles

Darya Klevetova, www.sxc.hu photo: Dixon

Volt Photo, www.sxc.hu photo: Harley

Dalia Drulia, www.sxc.hu photo: Sparky

Claudia Martinez, www.sxc.hu photo: Rolo

Eliya Selhub, www.flickr.com: Mr. Bean

Jen Ford, www.sxc.hu photo: Rufus

McCall Doyle Photography: Tonto, Whiskey

Matt Neely: Chuck

Mutts Matter Rescue: Homer

Beverly Lloyd-Roberts, www.sxc.hu photo: Comet

Steve Ekblad, www.sxc.hu photo: Wiggles

Renxx Gmdr, www.sxc.hu photo: Barney

Philip McKenzie, www.sxc.hu photo: Rascal

Sue Byford, www.sxc.hu photo: Spuds

Lost Dog Rescue: Irving

Monique Carboni: Dakota

Peter Pach, www.sxc.hu photo: Harry

Andrzej Pobiedzinski, www.sxc.hu photo: Max

Special thanks to:
Kim Houghton at Wag More Dogs (www.wagmoredogs.com)
Lost Dog Rescue (www.lostdogrescue.org)
Mutts Matter Rescue (www.muttsmatterrescue.com)